VERYMUCHWOW

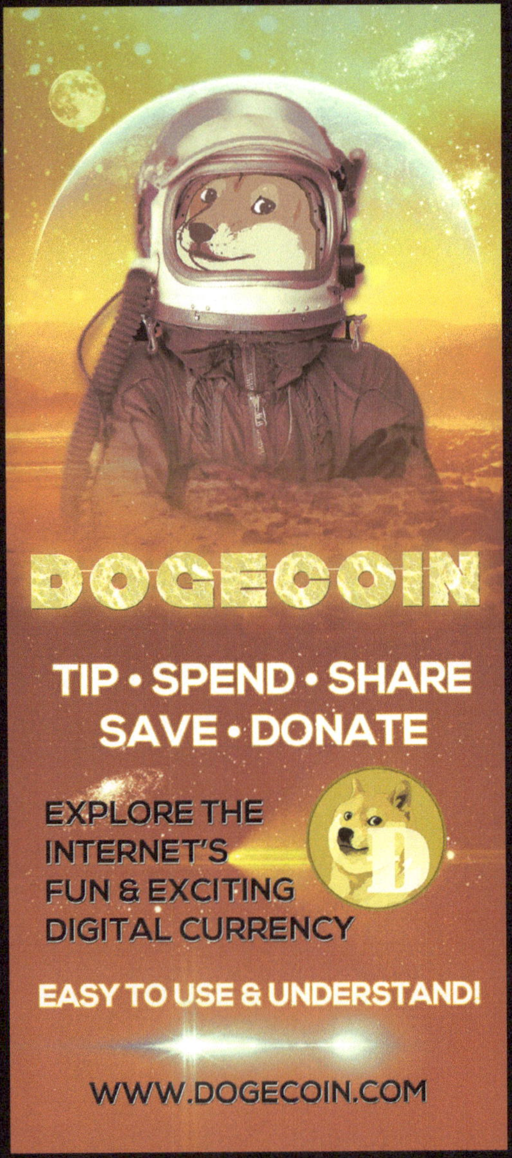

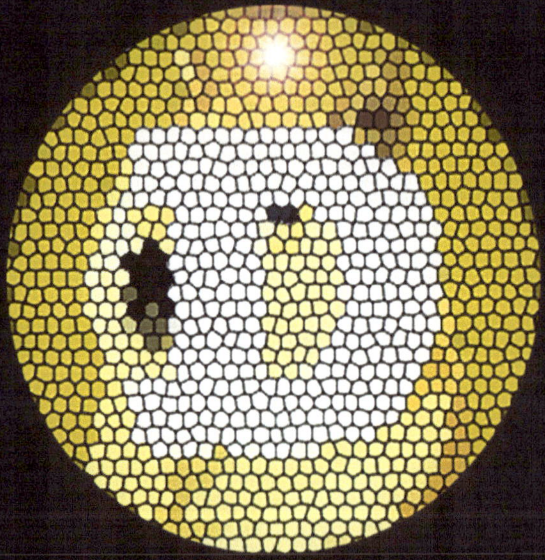

VERYMUCHWOW
WWW.VERYMUCHWOW.COM

BIRDIE JAWORSKI
EDITOR

Donations help keep VERY MUCH WOW alive!

Our Dogecoin Address is:
DQmDQT2GoqVZmXb18w27HS6oZecpf9p3Sa

All contributors, columnists, and artists
are paid in Dogecoin
for their submissions to VERY MUCH WOW.

Want to write for VMW?
Have art to share with VMW's audience?

Please contact:
editor@verymuchwow.com

ARTWORK CREDITS

All artwork in Very Much Wow is created
by the artists credited beneath each piece.
Other pieces are copyright Very Much Wow.

SHIBES LOVE FEEDBACK

info@verymuchwow.com

Published by:

VERY MUCH WOW
Albuquerque, New Mexico, USA
T 505 216 6187

TOM BOICE

Tom Boice is a regular contributor to CryptoCoinsNews.com, reporting on breaking news and spearheading their weekly Dogecoin addition. Holding a B.A. in English Literature from the University of West Florida, Tom has a passion for all things music and loves analyzing song composition. He currently lives in Pensacola, FL with his wife and enjoys helping out Sean's Outpost when possible.

tom@verymuchwow.com

CLAY MICHAEL GILLESPIE

Clay is an amateur writer of novels, short stories, poems and comic book scripts. His focus is on public relations. He has created and implemented strategic plans for Goodwill Industries of Central Indiana, Asian American Alliance of Indiana, Martin Luther King Jr. Dream Team, Digital Publishing Studios and Ball State University's Unified Student Media.

clay@verymuchwow.com

JYRO BLADE

Jyro is a video game programmer working in the New York City indie game development scene. He has been making games since he was 14 and some of his first memories involve playing Tetris on a classic GameBoy. He became involved with Doge in February 2014. Jyro enjoys DJing UK hardcore, skateboarding, and playing competitive Magic: The Gathering.

jyro@verymuchwow.com

EDGAR BOUNDS

Edgar once bought $10 dollar time-travel voucher service that claimed to deposit $9 of the $10 dollars in a fund to accumulate over the millennia, turning into a fortune that will be used when time-travel becomes viable to go back in time and rescue him. In retrospect this may have been somewhat of an ill-conceived purchase, though he did get a rush.

edgar@verymuchwow.com

AUTODOGE

autodoge is a designer, developer, and writer. He leads the Dogecoin development forum alongside the creator of dogetipbot and is a passionate advocate for the long-term future of cryptocurrency.

autodoge@verymuchwow.com

GOODSHIBE

GoodShibe is a passionate advocate for Dogecoin, a regular contributor to the /r/Dogecoin community and writer of the popular 'Of Wolves and Weasels' series – an archive of which can be found at goodshibe.com.

goodshibe@verymuchwow.com

SO TABLE MUCH CONTENTS

FEATURES

DOGECOIN BIZ

COMMUNITY

THE EDITOR

VERY MUCH WOW
THE DOGECOIN MAGAZINE

May 2014

A shibe and her Doge, Danté.

When I was a young girl, Neil Armstrong took his first step onto the surface of our moon. It's hard to believe today that the first moon journeys used slide rules, pencils, and stacks of paper more than computers. Since then, every time the moon rises full there is an exciting and new technology unleashed on the public.

My dad brought home an army green Micral when I was 8 years old, a monster machine much bigger and heavier than any household microwave today. I learned to create cute ASCII kittens, learned to program simple orders in FORTRAN, learned that everything in my life could be reduced to a Yes/No binary array. The screen was five inches across - if that - and my little FORTRAN art projects practically required a microscope to examine.

Since then, I have watched not only the change in computers and fashion and medical technology, but have experienced the wild ride of economic change, the transmission of balance by electron, by the very speed of light.

I discovered the world of cryptocurrency thanks to Dogecoin. Doge isn't just a silly dog on an imaginary coin. It is scientific dip into deep mathematics and encryption techniques. I started reading up on cryptography, learned how codes are used to keep our personal data safe. I read the Bitcoin White Paper by the still-elusive Satoshi Nakamoto. I remembered my love of FORTRAN and ASCII art, and signed up for a GitHub account. I even cloned and forked the Dogecoin code, and have been pouring through each new development. Dogecoin teaches me something new every day.

Dogecoin invites you into a world of education, experimentation, and adventure. Today you may see a silly dog on an imaginary coin, but in five years, you will be using Doge and other cryptocurrencies. In ten years, you will use nothing else. The world doesn't change in slow, ponderous ways. It jumps forward with each new discovery.

Cryptocurrency is one of those leaps. Today it is a leap of faith for users, but before you realize it, it will be everyday, mundane, something you use without thought.

Birdie

SHIBE GOOD

We were born out of laughter.

A flicker of creativity that would spark imaginations around the world.

Of course, no one knew that at the time.

Our creators, Jackson Palmer and Billy Markus - strangers, until a fortuitous meeting on IRC - would toil in the background putting the pieces together, but Dogecoin?

A silly Shiba Inu and her wry, goofy grin, pasted on a coin?

No less than a Mona Lisa for the Digital Age.

Okay, so, we were a joke - but we were a joke with four legs. A popular meme mixed with a healthy dose of Mammon... it was meant as a parody -- nobody expected it to work.

But what no one could have foreseen was that those who 'got' the joke would find the coin and build a home within it - form the beating heart behind it.

Dogecoin, with its tiny-but-active community - a smattering of fun, kind, compassionate people - stood in stark contrast to the 'serious business' of our Grandfather, Litecoin and Great Uncle Bitcoin.

"The 'friendly face of cryptos,' we're now over 75,000 strong and growing, daily. We are living proof that who we are, what we're doing, is working."

Our hoodies to their suits, we put a silly hat on naked profit and laughed at the notion.

Where some crypto enthusiasts shouted down 'stupid questions,' we encouraged everyone to learn with us. Where some left others to fend for themselves, we banded together and threw our money at each other with reckless abandon, celebrating raw creativity in all its forms.

From the start, we strived to be different. And, slowly, we began to attract like-minded souls.

More and more, our ranks swelled with, well, the kind of people who liked to joke about Dogecoin... and themselves. Smart, incisive, self-deprecating and yet self-aware, these folks were quickly awakening to the power granted to them by this digital coin.

As it turned out, our money could be used for more than just tips and game codes and gift cards. But where did it end? We began to experiment in earnest, to test our legs - what could we buy? What could we make happen?

As it turned out... not much. We struggled to find places who would accept our coins. And, so, in what would become something of a tradition, we made it a game.

We worked together, leveraged our fledgling community, to see who we could bring to the table. We signed petitions and sent flurries of emails and snuffled around for any hints of interest. Sure,

Tip GoodShibe ->

we went a bit overboard sometimes, got a tad excitable (sorry, Humble Bundle!) but our passion, our drive, it was infectious. We started making a name for ourselves, started getting attention -- some good, some bad.

Wolves and Weasels began poking around the edges of the lamplight, looking for DOGEs to snatch for themselves. A Christmas-time DogeWallet scam hurt us bad, and yet, almost immediately, we showed folks why we were different. For while other coins would smugly chortle at such misfortunes, within hours our fellow Shibes had rallied with a plan. A plan to reimburse the millions taken.

And from that plan came others - a Foundation was born and they worked

hard to further empower our community. Together, with their media savvy and our drive, we wasted little time in expanding our horizons. We began by helping to send Athletes to Sochi, then by giving Service Dogs to children with disabilities; followed it up by putting satellites into space and funding Science Research with our Doge coins. We built water wells in Kenya and then, for something completely different, we made friends with NASCAR and sponsored Josh Wise - a kind, talented, underdog, himself - to run a Dogecoin-themed car at Talladega, one of the most renowned races in the sport.

Bit by bit, day by day, we've found our stride. Each and every challenge overcome by choosing to laugh while we work.

And look how far we've come.

In the span of four months we've gone from a twinkle in our creators' eyes to the #3 digital currency in existence. The 'friendly face of cryptos,' we're now over 75,000 strong and growing, daily. We are living proof that who we are, what we're doing, is working.

Together, emboldened by our ethos of kindness, compassion and camaraderie, the Dogecoin community is showing the world a different way. An ideal that's not all that far off for all of us.

If we want it.

SHIBEMINT

An Interview with Tony of The Shibe Mint

by Birdie Jaworski

THE SHIBE MINT
SMB
IN DOGE WE TRUST

**You can't hold a Dogecoin.
Or can you?**

Dogecoins, like all cryptocurrencies, can be difficult for the walletless to understand. They are imaginary, just a figment of coded imagination on the blockchain. I keep trying to explain this to my best friend.

"So when I download my Doge, they are sitting in my computer, right? There's a wallet in there, and the coins are in the wallet."

She looks at me with one hand on mouse, one on hip, as if I should nod my head, but my eyes and grin freeze and I look like a human shibe in a black t-shirt imprinted with a cartoon shibe. I often find myself in these Escher-esque moments when I talk Doge.

It's a mind-bender. The wallet is a symbol, is a way for us to accept the idea that we own pieces of something that only exist because we choose to give a bit of nothing value. It's kind of like the Velveteen Rabbit, I've found myself explaining more than once when someone asks me why I keep wishing them to the moon. We believe in Doge, we love Doge, we wish Doge real, and Doge becomes alive in response.

Even when you state it as simple and plainly as you can, it sounds as silly as a dog on a coin. So I did what every shibe should do when faced with explaining the unexplainable. I bought a few Dogecoins from *The Shibe Mint*.

Tony Pepperoni - hey, we're talking about dogs on coins that only exist because we believe, so the names you see slung around Doge circles have a certain poetic certainty - runs The Shibe Mint. He discovered Dogecoin the way many of us did - through a search to understand the concept of cryptocurrency.

"Every year I come up with a 'holiday project' to make productive use of my time," he explains. "This year my project was to learn about cryptocurrency - how it works, how to mine, how to trade. In my search for knowledge, I heard about this new upstart coin that was gaining a lot of attention from a passionate community and was quickly hooked."

Tony turned his new obsession into a business making physical Dogecoins that a person can touch, hold, and keep in their pocket.

The coins are roughly the size and thickness of a silver half-dollar and come in copper and a full ounce of fine silver. The face of the coin is the beloved Shiba Inu staring enigmatically into space with the word WOW in beveled metal across her cheek.

My silver Shibe Mint 100 Dogecoin beauty, resting in the New Mexican desert / photos by Birdie

The coins mimic the official logo with the "shibe speak" running along the border: wow - much coin - how money - so crypto - plz mine. The back of the coin is the Dogecoin "D," the year, and the Dogecoin "value" of the coin stamped into the metal. Of course, the value of One Doge will always be One Doge, but it's fun to hold a silver coin and wonder.

"We first come up with a product idea - in this case the first copper Dogecoin - and a design," Tony explains. "The design is used to create a die - the mold that is used to stamp the blank coins. Finally we need to get the blank coins in and run them through the machines that stike the coins with the die."

The Shibe Mint has customers from across the globe. Half of Tony's orders come from the United States, followed by Canada and Australia.

"We love seeing a new country show up on an order!" Tony grins.

Tony has most been surprised by The Shibe Mint's success.

"We thought it would be a good idea, because of the growing and passionate community," he says. "But we didn't expect it to take off as it has. It's been a very pleasant surprise. There is a pretty big lead time from concept to ship date, and I will never forget having to pay for all that silver after being in operation for about a week - it was a pretty big leap of faith."

The concept of a physical coin that represents a cryptocurrency was first established by the Cassacius coin company with their physical Bitcoin.

"There is something about having a tangible item that represents the digital currency that I'm such a big fan of," Tony muses. "I carry one on me everywhere I go, for luck, to use as a prop in a dis cussion about either dogecoin or the Shibe Mint and to make 50/50 decisions. From day 1, the question I asked myself was - if I wasn't making these, would I buy one? The answer is a resounding yes."

Tony's customers use their physical Dogecoins to spread the word about Doge. Some tweet photos of their coins to their online followers. Others have posted YouTube videos. Of course, the coins have been incredibly popular on the Dogecoin subReddit.

"It has been overwhelming," Tony says. "I would love for a Shibe Mint coin to make it to the moon one day. I know that a few teams are looking to get as close as we can for now - and we are thrilled to be a small part of that."

For Tony, the moon means mass acceptance in Dogecoin.

"We are building towards that," he predicts, "with an increase in value to reward the early believers. We are excited to be on the rocketship."

Buy your own copper and silver Dogecoins at The Shibe Mint: www.shibemint.com

Đ
TO
THE
MOON

DOGE2048

There are many variations of the popular puzzle game 2048, by Gabriele Cirulli, available to play for free today. However, this "Doge-ified" version, by Tiny Mammals, contains by far the most Doge per serving.

In the original 2048, players slide numbered tiles around on a 4 by 4 grid. Players can either use WASD, arrow keys, or swipe on a mobile platform to move all tiles on the grid in the chosen direction. When two tiles of the same value touch, they merge into a single tile with a combined value of the two. In this way, a 4 tile sliding into another 4 tile gives a single 8 tile; pairing that 8 with another 8 gives you a 16, and so on. Play continues until the board completely fills and there are no identical tiles that can be merged.

DOGE2048 replaces these numerically valued tiles with a variety of animated doge faces with various backgrounds. There are a total of eleven unique doge faces to merge including the simple doge with a turquoise background, the rainbow doge, and the doge with the pepperoni pizza spinning behind it.

This version also removes the bland, beige wallpaper of the original game and instead smoothly cycles through a rainbow of colors as a backdrop. As you pair tiles, you are rewarded with encouraging word pop-ups such as "so scoring" and "such playing." Needless to say, the font of choice for all text is Comic Sans.

From a gameplay standpoint, DOGE2048 plays exactly the same as its parent. Nothing has been changed except for the visuals. Tiny Mammals certainly did not need to change anything, as this very simple mechanic of pairing tiles is unbelievably addictive. I personally find DOGE2048 a lit-

tle more difficult than the original, simply because the Doge tiles are a little harder to intuitively recognize compared to the numbered tiles. The original 2048 has become somewhat of a sensation in its short lifespan, so keeping the gameplay identical feels familiar to players of the original and allows the silliness of the graphics to stand on their own.

Perhaps the only major issue I noticed with DOGE2048 is the mobile platform capability. The original 2048 performs quite well on both a Windows phone and an iPod Touch and has very little latency or missed inputs when connected to a strong Wifi signal. DOGE2048, however, tends to have a major delay on an iPod and does not receive inputs at all on the same Windows phone. These issues are not present when playing on a desktop using keyboard input.

DOGE2048 has become one of my most frequented bookmarks recently and I can't help but return to the game over and over again. I find the doge version provides just enough added stimulation and familiarity, given my affinity for doges, to retain my attention over the original. It may not be the best choice for mobile users, but perhaps your device will perform better on the site than either of the tested ones did.

I highly recommend trying out DOGE2048 for yourself, just don't expect to get anything productive done for an hour or so after you do.

Check out DOGE2048 at
www.doge2048.com

Tip Jyro ->

"DOGE2048 has become one of my most frequented bookmarks recently and I cant help but return to the game over and over again."

Spread Your Wealth
18 EASY WAYS TO
'cause those coins ain't gonna share themselves...

On Wagging Your Tail in Public

Like most other shibes, I love to give my Dogecoins away. Sometimes my coins find their way to a charity. Sometimes I tip another shibe for a funny or kind comment. The rest of the time, I give my coins away to the unsuspecting public. In the time that Dogecoin has existed, I have turned 37 people - none of whom had ever heard about cryptocurrency or had perhaps had only heard the name "Bitcoin" - into shibes. That number is probably higher; it represents only the people who contacted me after their dip into Doge.

You have to keep in mind the Golden Doge Rule: There is a fine line between evangelism and flat-out crazy talk. (I fail at this, alas...)

If you are intelligent and discerning, taking an approach that invites a person to tell you about Dogecoin will serve you and the community well. Instead of launching into a sales pitch, why not ask the person you meet, "I've been following the cryptocurrency market - things like Dogecoin and Bitcoin - and wonder if you've heard anything about them."

Such an opening will allow you to correct (gently, please) any misconceptions that someone may have. And more times that not, I am willing to bet that you will be surprised, even enlightened, by the answers you receive.

Everyone wants to be a Dogecoin evangelist. Why not be a quiet zen master of the market?

Here are 18 ways to pique someone's interest in Dogecoin. You may think these ways are silly, even ridicu-lous. You may think that your potential shibe has a more technologically sophisticated palate. But the truth is that we are all human, all with the same basic needs, and an approach that doesn't rock a person's ideological boat is often times the most effective. A marketing approach needs to be as silly and gentle as the coin.

Most of the world doesn't follow cutting-edge technological advances like cryptocurrencies. They are more likely to discover Dogecoin through a friend, family member, or coworker than they are to find themselves in the Reddit Dogecoin sub. Sometimes a person needs to hear about something like Dogecoin multiple times

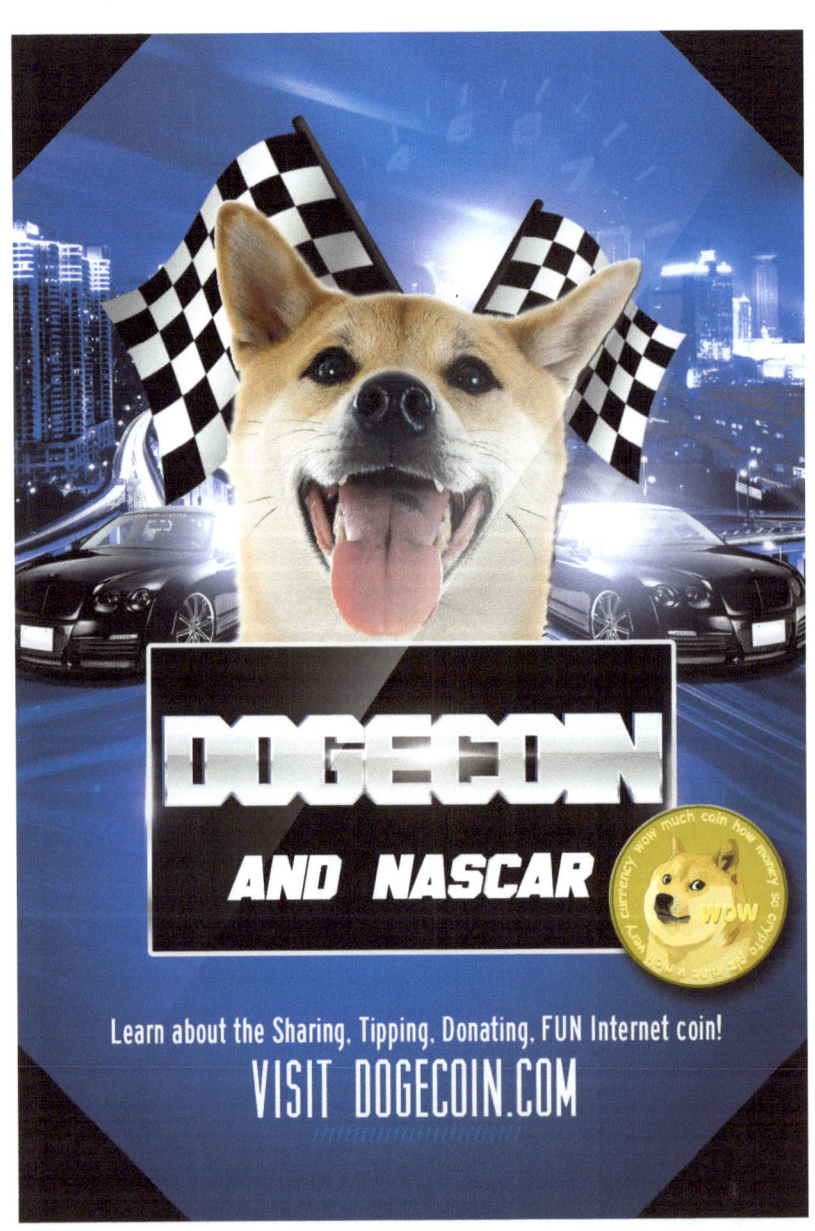

Learn about the Sharing. Tipping. Donating. FUN Internet coin!
VISIT DOGECOIN.COM

share & promote
DOGECOIN

Simple and effective ways - beyond our wonderful tipping bots - to share Dogecoins!

before they feel comfortable enough to look into it.

Most of these suggestions utilized paper Dogecoin wallets. These are fun and easy to make! You can print out a colorful template and add your own public and private address at a site like *www.firstcointact.com*, or you can simply hand people a postcard with an invitation to connect with you in order to receive their Dogecoins. I have used both methods effectively.

When handing out paper wallets, I put an expiration date on them. I ask the receiver to contact me through my email or telephone number prior to that date, and if the date has passed when they find the wallet, to call me for a new one. When I am contacted, I scratch that wallet off of my master list; it now belongs to a pup who will learn and grow along with the rest of us! If the expiration date comes and goes without a call, I will remove the Dogecoins from the wallet's address and load a new wallet. You never have to feel that you are "throwing away" your Dogecoins.

Enjoy these simple ways to share Dogecoin with others! The moon will be a lonely place without them!

- Birdie

STICKERS AND BUTTONS
Make or purchase Dogecoin stickers and buttons. Stick them on your outgoing bills, your bumper, your best friend's butt! Visual recognition, psychologists will tell you, happens before intellectual recognition.

FUNDRAISERS
Does your favorite charitable organization need to raise funds? As our community has seen, shibes are generous with their time, talent, and Doge. Ask the Dogecoin PR team for help!

OPTIMIZE YOUR EMAIL
Do you have a signature beneath each message you send via text or email? Why not add your Dogecoin address? Beneath your address, add an invitation to learn what that crazy string of numbers and letters means.

WEAR YOUR DOGE
Some of our shibe designers are posting awesome tee shirts that feature Dogecoin in a variety of ways. Why not add a shirt to your wardrobe? I have several - a happy I Heart Dogecoin tee, and another that says "I use Dogecoin and I vote."

TIP • SPEND
DOGECOINS
DONATE • SHARE

Tip every waitstaff person, musician, hair stylist, bartender, and newspaper delivery girl with Dogecoins in addition to their traditional fiat-based gratuity.

Do you like to write? Consider pitching a regular cryptocurrency column to your local paper or workplace newsletter. You can cover the news surrounding Dogecoin, from the latest exchange rates to new merchants accepting Doge in your area to a roundup of featured news stories from around the globe.

The media "eats" content. The daily paper has to fill their pages - online or in print - with relevant, interesting content. Dogecoin has made news in the major outlets thanks to the Jamaican Bobled and NASCAR intiatives. Show the editor some of these stories, and explain that you can bring a local touch to crypto coverage. Q and A columns can be popular, too.

IS THERE A MEETUP GROUP IN YOUR CITY DEVOTED TO OUR FAVORITE CRYPTO?! START ONE!

Meetups are a great way to introduce like-minded individuals to crypto, especially our beloved Dogecoin!

In addition, Dogecoin Meetups will open the opportunity to meet other Shibes in the "wild."

Be sure to draft a clear and precise statement that explains exactly what your Meetup is about. Break it down so that people will understand what type of conversations you hope to develop surrounding Dogecoin.

Once you decide to put a Meetup event on the calendar make sure you announce it and give yourself some time to promote the event so that people can RSVP.

INSTAGRAM, FACEBOOK, TWEET, YOUTUBE, REDDIT, VINE, AND BLOG YOUR DOGECOIN PURCHASES

Buy a burger with Doge? Order a few bars of custom-made soap with your coins? Take a video or photo of every Dogecoin purchase you make and upload them to your favorite social media sites.

Make sure you mention the ease of the transaction:

"Wow! I just ordered six boxes of Green Tea Kit Kats from Japan and it took less than a second using Dogecoins!"

Social media allows you to build relationships with people who are curious about Dogecoin but afraid to jump into establish communities like Reddit. Strike up a conversation with your followers, and encourage them to ask you questions.

SHARE COPIES OF THE DOGECOIN MAGAZINE...
VERY MUCH WOW!

Leave a copy of Very Much Wow in your dentist's office, library, auto repair waiting area, place of work, day care center, laundrymat, coffee shop, ANYWHERE that people need some

VERY MUCH WOW!

DEMONSTRATE

A few weeks ago I held a Dogecoin demonstration at my Community College. I invited other women who were returning to school - like me. Most of these women have family in Latin America, so I handed out invitations in Spanish.

I was able to get six women online and set up with a Dogecoin wallet.

SPONSOR A TEAM

How about sponsoring a Little League Team? Many community teams look for sponsors who can help them get uniforms, snacks, or space for their games. The Dogecoin logo looks great on a baseball shirt!

GONE TO THE DOGS

I've been using the money I earmark from my paycheck to sponsor dogs at the local Humane Society shelter. I donate to the shelter using Dogecoins - they are now invested in Doge - along with a big box of healthy dog treats.

The dogs look forward to my visit, and the shelter gets to collect and save Dogecoins in order to help them build a new wing to their facility.

I have had several shelter workers ask about Dogecoin and how they can get involved.

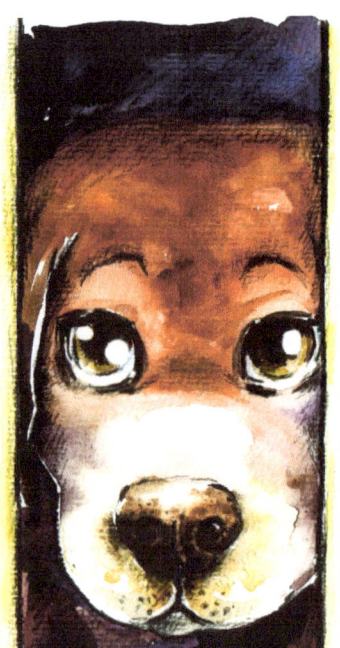

EMAIL EDITOR@VERYMUCHWOW.COM

ONE MERCHANT A WEEK

Commit to asking one merchant each week if they accept Dogecoins? If not, tell them that others in the community are starting to accept Doge, and ask if you can help them step into 2014! Just one a week makes a difference.

ART + DOGE = WOW

My city has a once-a-month art crawl. Galleries and studios open their doors to art lovers over the course of the evening. Many of these shows need sponsors to help defray the costs of the opening: wine, cheese, postcards.

Sponsor an art show or an artist. Or, ask a gallery to hold a Dogecoin Art show!

Dogecoin is the perfect payment vector for artists; they can receive commissions from around the world, and help grow a following in the Doge community.

FLASH MOB

Invite your friends to practice a fun dance, play, or song that involves Dogecoin and spring it on the unsuspecting public. Mall food courts or public parks are great places to find a crowd. Hand out paper wallets filled with Dogecoin at the end! VERY MUCH WOW will pay a 50K Dogecoin bounty to the 1st person to post their successful public Dogecoin flash mob on YouTube!

DOGE PARTY!!!

Hey, it's almost summer! Why not organize a Doge Days of August party? Or a Canine Conundrum bash? The key is to have a mix of guests   a solid handful of Dogecoin enthusiasts, and a good number of people who have no idea what a Doge is. Set up stations around the party where people can sign up for a wallet, watch some of the awesome Dogecoin videos, and hold a "Make Your Own Paper Wallet" contest - winner gets 1000 Doge!

CRYPTO CLASS FOR KIDS

Today's younger folks are the people who will be using cryptocurrency without thought in the near future. Offer to set up a workshop after school at the local high school. They've already been on Reddit - why not introduce them to the Dogecoin sub and give them a wallet?

WOW MUCH TALK

ROSSNICOLL

I first noticed Ross Nicoll on the Dogecoin subReddit. He wrote with a simple and elegant authority. I was still in the Dogecoin Honeymoon phase, though, and I didn't want to read comments that questioned the code, the underlying framework of my latest obsession.

I kept coming back to a threaded series of his comments; there was something behind his words that intrigued me. Others that had gripes with the coin's development used bombastic language, attempted to spread gasoline while holding a lit match. Not Ross. He used the language of science to illustrate his thoughts, to gently correct commenters - like me - who thought they knew it all.

Because of Ross, I joined GitHub and forked the code. I wanted to watch the chaos of crypto code,

wanted to be able to discuss Dogecoin's finer points with the same kind of finesse and beauty. I won't ever reach Ross' level of expertise, of course. I won't ever come close. But Ross has handed me a quantum leap in my own understanding, and after reading his answers to our questions, I'm sure you will feel the same.

- Birdie

VM**W:** When did you first learn about Dogecoin? What did you think? Why did you get involved? Do you mine?

RN: I heard about Dogecoin first in mid-December; I was reading on reddit about how BTC China had announced it wouldn't be taking any further deposits of yuan, and Bitcoin's price had crashed as a result. There was a comment about

Dogecoin, and looked up the Wikipedia entry out of curiosity. One of the things I disagreed with in Bitcoin's design was the relatively small number of coins, and the idea that there would be 100 billion Dogecoin intrigued me, and I started digging further.

As with many others I got my first few Dogecoin as a tip. I'd been involved in Bitcoin to a degree from around 2011-2013, and wanted to get involved with cryptocurrencies again, and the idea of getting in at the start (or thereabouts) of an exciting new coin really appealed to me. I have tried mining, however as I don't really have space for mining gear, and need my main desktop PC much of the time, it's generally simpler for me to simply buy cryptocurrencies via exchanges.

DOGE By the #s

Year of Birth

2013

That's nearly 4 years old in Dog Years!

Current Client Version

1.7

Better than Bitcoin, Yo!

VALUE

1 Đ = 1 Đ

What else matters, shibe?!

"I want to see Dogecoin enable sole traders to easily accept payments with minimal fuss, and to cut down on costs for anyone sending money to friends and family, irrespective of international borders."

lonewolfgame.com

DEVELOPER DOGE

VMW: You have been contributing to the current developments at the Dogecoin repository at GitHub. What are the biggest issues that contributors are trying to solve or implement?

RN: Obviously we've had a rapid sequence of Dogecoin client releases recently, as we've moved from Litecoin 0.6, to 0.8, then reworked the mining specification to mitigate impact of multipools on the mining difficulty - with help from DigiByte. Right now, my main priority is to provide a rock-solid base for later changes, while also trying to avoid required updates and the work they require for our community. The upcoming 1.7 client is based on the Bitcoin 0.9 client - moving away from Litecoin, although keeping Scrypt for mining, and we're currently performing extensive testing on it to ensure it's as stable as it possibly can be.

Looking onwards to 1.8 and beyond, there's is of course the question of how to deal with ASICs, and their impact on both the mining community and the security of the coin. Personally my main priorities are foundational; I'm intending to write up some of the protocols in use by Dogecoin as RFCs (Request For Comments) for submission to the IETF (Internet Engineering Task Force), to provide extensively documented and reviewed references for Dogecoin. I'm also hoping to work with the Bitcoin developers on the architecture of the client, to enable easier separation of presentation and business logic layers.

VMW: Tell readers about ASICs.

RN: ASICs are a frequent topic of discussion with the developers, and naturally we're considering every option. In an ideal world they would be a solution to the excessive power requirements of current approaches to mining, however right now of course their adoption raises understandable concerns from our mining community who have in many cases made extensive investment in GPU hardware. A number of ideas have been proposed for changing the proof of work algorithm, at the cost of a further hard-fork of the blockchain.

We have to balance these risks, and the potential for introducing a serious bug in critical code if we were to make such a change, against the costs of inaction. Regrettably most suggested solutions

for ASIC-resistant proof of work merely delay the issue, and essentially leave us in a technology arms-race with ASIC manufacturers. For now, we're actively discussing merged-mining with other coins, as Jackson Palmer suggested in his recent reddit post, and will continue to evaluate the situation.

VMW: How important has community involvement been in making positive changes in the Dogecoin core code?

RN: I'm very grateful for the confidence shown in myself and the other developers by the community, but yes we absolutely depend on their contributions to help us make decisions which will impact Dogecoin. I do actively read /r/dogecoin as well as other subreddits, and take on board a lot of concerns and discussion. As much as is possible I also try to engage with discussions in the developer channel on IRC, and changes in direction based on feedback is perhaps more common than I'd like to admit!

VMW: Is it just a silly dog on a coin?

RN: Of course not! Being a meme based cryptocurrency is absolutely a huge part of our identity, but it's what draws us together, it's not all of what is Dogecoin. To me the image represents our willingness both to be friendly and approachable, and not take ourselves too seriously. It's often the first thing new community members see of the coin, and I think it helps shape their perceptions of us all.

VMW: Where do you see Dogecoin in 1 year? How about in 5 years? Do you think you will continue to stay involved in the development end?

RN: A year from now, I'd like to see Dogecoin as well recognized name not just amongst cryptocurrency fans, but also the general public. We're currently rapidly expanding our adoption amongst merchants, and I would expect that Dogecoin acceptance will be moving along at a rapid pace. From a technical stance I'd look for us to have an improved selection of wallet software, based around a common core, with different user interfaces to satisfy different use-cases (home, professional, point of sale, etc.)

Five years from now, I'd look to have an established Dogecoin economy where converting to/from traditional currencies is an unusual thing to do. The entire cryptocurrency landscape is likely to be very different by then, with the big-name coins widely accepted in the same way most companies accept major credit cards now. With an increasing blockchain size, mining will be transforming from an issue of processing power, to one of disk space and bandwidth to handle transaction volume. What are currently next-generation coins such as Ethereum will be well established by this point, and I would imagine we'll be evaluating technologies for potential integration into the coin.

I'd absolutely hope I'll still be involved with Dogecoin in the long term, although realistically have to concede it will depend on demands on my time.

VMW: How can persons new to Dogecoin get involved in the development end?

RN: The best advice I can give anyone wanting to get involved is to find something you're good at and just do it. Developers can submit pull requests with changes through Github, and certainly that's how I got started. We also always need others to help with testing, documentation, community co-ordination and a hundred other tasks. Dropping by the #dogecoin-dev IRC channel on Freenode is an excellent first step for anyone unsure where to start.

VMW: What does "The Moon" mean to you?

RN: I suppose I see "The Moon" as the point at which Dogecoin has an impact on the world not just through its community's charitable works, but also as a technology for transforming the movement of money. I want to see Dogecoin enable sole traders to easily accept payments with minimal fuss, and to cut down on costs for anyone sending money to friends and family, irrespective of international borders. It may surprise many people, but I don't see cryptocurrencies as an alternative to banks, instead I want to see the two competing and in doing so improving finance for everyone.

JOE SHARP

JOE SHARP OF DOGEFORSALE.COM TALKS DOGE, DOGE, AND DOGE!

One of the biggest challenges to universal Dogecoin adoption is the reality that the cute coins have been difficult to obtain if you don't mine. Larger cryptocurrency exchanges have been reluctant to add Doge to their roster, and those that have - until recently - required that a user first purchase and use Bitcoins to complete the transaction.

Joe Sharp talked to Very Much Wow over Skype about **DogeForSale.com** - a peer-to-peer Dogecoin exchange in London that enables Doge buyers and sellers to trade in a safe, Escrow-enhanced environment.

Joe grinned as he talked. His hair fell into his face. He broke into an even bigger smile. He sounded approachable, kind, intelligent, with a twist of imp. He began his story at the same place many early Doge adopters start: he discovered Bitcoin first.

"I worked for a publishing company. I saw something on Wired.com that a publisher was the first of its kind to accept Bitcoin. I had heard it mentioned by a couple of my friends," he explained, "but it was more of this dark underside of things."

Joe bought some Bitcoin. His first purchase took place at a local pub. He bought a pint of beer and a packet of crisps.

"It took about half-an-hour to process because of the block-chain," he laughed. "I offered to pay in cash, but it eventually went through. It was the most expensive pint and crisps I've ever bought, as Bitcoin price rose and that pint ended up costing 50-60 pounds."

Joe leaned toward his computer and stared into the screen. He started talking about Dogecoin. He looked like the coin's muse, with wide eyes and an enigmatic expression.

"I tried to get my company to accept Bitcoin and did a few presentations. I guess they are a big, busy company, and they didn't have time to look into it," he explained. "My friend Dan [Tudor, lead developer at DogeForSale.com - ed.] said that he built this Dogecoin exchange thing, and he invited me on board. We launched in early February."

Visitors to DogeForSale.com will find a clean and easy-to-navigate design. Clear links invite the interested to learn how to buy or sell Dogecoins. A list of current offers populates the center of the home page, with a seller's pricing and rating next to each name.

"It *IS* a silly dog on a coin," Joe laughed. "People can relate to it. The dog takes the fear out of cryptocurrency. Jackson Palmer came out with the concept. The inter-net loves these things. I think it's good."

DogeForSale.com is still in

JOE SHARP OF DOGEFORSALE.COM

its formative stages, Joe said. The goal is to create a user-friendly and safe marketplace for Dogecoin buyers and sellers.

"One of the most interesting trades involved a kid in South Africa," Joe said. "During school, he sent us an email asking for Dogecoin. He did a bank transfer at school. He's been in Dogecoin ever since. Our site enables people to buy Dogecoin directly, people who might not have been able to in the past."

Joe rested his head in one hand. He stared into space as if he were contemplating the Great Shibe.

"There's this whole Doge-world community," he mused.

"I feel so strongly about this dog on a coin. I'm not a fan of the pump-and-dumps," he said, describing the practice of mining Dogecoin in order to immediately sell it in the marketplace for Bitcoin.

"A lot of people think that Dogecoin is cheap," he added, "but it's a relatively stable currency."

Joe said that the company was trying to figure out how to sell car insurance for Dogecoin, prompting both of us to explode in laughter. Only with Dogecoin can such a mundane purchase seem absurd, beautiful, and alien all at once.

However, the business side of Dogecoin often seems at odds with the well-publicized charity campaigns where Doge has been used to fund safe water wells in Africa as well as send the famous Jamaican bobsled Olympic athletes to Sochi for the Winter Games.

"We need to stay solid with the Dogecoin Foundation," Joe cautioned. "That's the cornerstone of what it stands for, and everything can grow around it."

Joe held his phone to the computer and showed me a cute video of a local woman trying to pronounce **Dogecoin**. She didn't recognize the name or the Doge, but she gave it a good try. "*Dog-gie-coin?*"

"I love that," he said. "I love seeing real people interact with Doge. There's a Shiba Inu

photography group on Facebook and they love talking about their dogs."

DogeForSale.com recently hired two interns, and is focusing on digital strategies and development, but Joe stays focused on the fact that Dogecoin is uniting people across the globe in unexpected and charming ways.

"We're on different sides of the world, and we're both talking about a dog on a coin," he laughed.

What's the next fun project for DogeForSale.com?

"We'd love to do 'A Day in the Life of a Doge,'" he explained. "But we need to find a Doge first."

-Birdie

Ðogecoin

WATCH ME REVIEW

CLAY MICHAEL GILLESPIE

Photos courtesy of Marvel Comics and Sony Pictures with a twist of VMW artistic manipulation

Captain America Shows that Phase Two is Much Darker than Expected

> "It honestly makes you question how much control Disney really has over Marvel at this point, which in my opinion is a good thing."

Steve Rogers has returned with his shield as Captain America yet again, and this time it's personal. As cliché as it sounds, the saying holds quite a bit of merit if you've only seen the trailer for Captain America: The Winter Soldier. Buy a ticket for the movie. I can promise you that your presumptions on the plot are way off.

The movie's plot hits very close to home around the topics of surveillance, social media and government control, which in turn changes it into a Marvel movie that fans have not become accustomed to. This whole journey, Captain America has been learning about this new digital age, and he's pissed off with how S.H.E.I.L.D. is handling business.

Captain America seems to fuel every punch with the deep-seated anger he holds inside. He may be the "good-boy, golden child", but somehow every time he hits someone with his shield, smashes through a wall

or even fist-fights with MMA fighter George St. Pierre, you feel it in your bones. However the audio was constructed for those gripping moments is nothing short of fascinating, as it's not something Marvel has been able to achieve until now. Even the Hulk didn't make you shake in your seat as he ripped apart the Chitauri army in The Avengers, and he's at least four times the size of Cap.

Not only can you feel it when Cap makes a hit, you feel it when the mysterious Winter Soldier makes a kill. Each brutal (and yes, they are brutal) killing The Winter Soldier achieves is met with quite a bit of shock as it honestly makes you question how much control Disney really has over Marvel at this point, which in my opinion is a good thing.

The main boys aren't the only ones with strength though. Black Widow really shows how much of a badass she can be as she fights her way through thug after thug. Her fighting style was impressive and very well portrayed, but I would be remiss if I didn't mention her lack of character development. Yes, while she has been in Iron Man 2 and The Avengers, it would have been nice of the writers to work in a bit more character development as she fought alongside the star-spangled Avenger.

Falcon seems to get this similar treatment, but it's to be expected with this being his first introduction into the MCU. It just seemed as Widow's dialogue was twisted to the "stereotypical girl" type, and less on the "hardcore, amazing, oh-my-god-did-she-just-do-that" sort of thing that most fans get from the other heroes (Hawkeye excluded, due to his lack of character development at all).

However, the plot is intricate. Like, really intricate. The Winter Soldier isn't the only Marvel villain to have a hand in Cap's troubles. The brains behind the operation are that of someone from Cap's past that true Marvel fans will be very pleased to watch make his famed appearance. In a monologue about surveillance and social media, he echoes all of the fears we the people currently hold against the NSA now in the real world. It's a chilling realization to say the least, and truly honest writing.

And before you make assumptions, no, it's not Robert Redford's character Alexander Pierce, who in the trailer is seen to put Cap in a conflicting position. I told you before; your presumptions on the plot are way off. But if you're a movie buff, watch what's inside Pierce's fridge and see if you can find the underlying meaning connected to Redford's acting past. There's a bit of an Easter egg hidden there just for you.

That being said about villains, The Winter Soldier character is built very well. He's creepy, scary and a formidable opponent to Captain America, Falcon and Black Widow with a sweet metal arm. He's got a troubled past too, that was obviously well planned in the MCU by the fantastic writing team. The entire movie, The Winter Soldier maintains your interest as to where he will go and what he will do next. Will Cap beat him? Or is he way too strong? That's what most important when watching a villain. They don't just have to be formidable; they also have to keep you guessing.

Previously, I enjoyed Thor: The Dark World immensely. I now realize why. The plot was darker than what's previously been showcased in Phase One. Now that I've seen Captain America: The Winter Soldier, I realize that Mar-

vel is done trying to get their foot in the door and they're ready to capitalize on the serious story-progression they've been planning all along. I look forward to Guardians of the Galaxy, and can't wait to see how the rest of Phase 2 progresses.

Tip Clay:

TIPPING THE LIGHT FANTASTIC

Chester eyes the camera while Josh Mohland discusses the finer points of Dogecoin tipping

I started mining Doge with my old computer; a machine as slow and ponderous and as filled with arcane knowledge as its owner. I starting mining because I thought I make some money, might be able to quit my minimum wage job at a corporate mega-mart. But Dogecoin is no Bitcoin, no November '13 ticket on a bullet train. My 7 Kh/s didn't hand me a retirement fund. It didn't even hand me a nice dinner out. But Dogecoin gave me something better, something I never anticipated: a million reasons to care about something and someone else.

Dogecoin didn't make itself happen, despite the coin's adorable mascot and early mining ease. It has become The Internet Currency by way of a million small handshakes filled with the invisible coins, by way of friendship and shared smile, by the gracious motion of appreciative finger against keyboard. Dogecoin has become bigger than the meme itself, a representation of charity and love wrapped in Comic Sans, thanks in large part to the phenomenon of tipping.

The guru of tipping is, of course, **Josh Mohland**, whose **Dogetipbot** pushed the once-joke coin onto a spaceship and aimed it at the moon.

I spoke with Josh over Skype while his cat, Chester, paced back and forth in the background.

Josh found Dogecoin through the Bitcointalk.org forum, and decided to mine a million Dogecoins for laughs.

"I was going to mine a million Doge," he explains. "Then I thought I would do three million. I told a couple of friends about it, sent a bunch of Doge to them, and here I am."

Josh still mines, with a couple of rigs providing a warm spot for Chester to sleep. He started Dogetipbot in response to a community request.

"I was on the Dogecoin subReddit," he remembers. "It started out with a post. I said that I could do that, and it literally took off overnight."

Dogetipbot averages between a million and two million tips a day, some days reaching much higher when a charity or promotions drive is in gear. For Josh, Dogetipbot has become an official fulltime job, but it started out as an all-hours venture between keeping the bot running, fixing bugs and crashes, and eventually rewriting the entirety of the code.

"We wanted to move it beyond Reddit," Josh says, "but none of the sites as of yet have the volume that Reddit has."

Josh points out that some of the tipping sprees on Twitter - such as those involving enigmatic shibe, SaveThemHood, have resulted in enormous donations. His company, Wow Such Business, Inc., plans to stick to tipping.

"It's what we're good at. We're sticking with it.

JOSH MOHLAND

"For a cryptocurrency making fun of all of the alt coins, it has achieved a life of its own. It has value; it's super approachable."

Why mess with what works?" Josh adds.

I asked Josh if Dogecoin was just a silly dog on a coin. Chester looked at the camera that moment as if to nod, Why yes, of course.

"It's both," Josh laughs. For a cryptocurrency making fun of all of the alt coins, it has achieved a life of its own. It has value; it's super approachable. It has a huge fan base on Reddit."

Josh loves the lightheartedness of the community, the willingness of complete strangers to post funny photoshopped pictures of Shiba Inus as President, rap star, and economic genius.

"We are so ridiculous," he grins. "We throw money at people on the internet. You get to throw change at people on the internet! Our median tip value is 2.7 cents, and yet we have days when we're throwing several thousand dollars around. The unit bias is what Dogecoin has going for it, even if it is a fraction of a cent."

Josh's best Dogetipbot story falls back into deep Doge history, in other words, a few months ago in mid December 2013.

"Most people don't remember this," he cautions. "It was the X Prize contest with a 10 million Doge bounty."

The prize promised to award the first cryptocurrency tipbot with over 10K users the grand prize.

"At that time, we were growing like crazy. We had around 500 users and were hoping to reach 1000. Not even Bitcoin had that many tippers," Josh reminisces. "The bot was buggy and crashing a lot. We never thought we would reach 1000 let alone 10K. Today we're at over 54K users and growing every day."

Dogetipbot serves anywhere from 500-1000 active tippers a day. The recipients end up in the 2-3000 number. More people receive than give, but the action of seeing shibes continue to tip, even when they are tipping the very last of their Doge, inspires new users to take a hard look at community values and ethics.

Josh tells me that January 2014 was somehow a huge month, despite the value of Dogecoin rising to new heights.

"It's funny, January was our huge month. We saw tipping when the value was high; in fact, it was the reverse of what you'd expect. January was a massive amount for us," he says. "The volume was off the charts."

Josh's first computer was an Apple IIe, thanks to his dad. He has a background in IT and backend management. He began his work life in technical support and man

Continued on next page >>>

agement, and anyone interacting with him at the Dogecoin subReddit has to admit that he's developed a gentle style and a kind and expert way of dealing with critics.

The Dogecoin client has recently been upgraded to version 1.7, which makes Josh laugh.

"Not even Bitcoin is at 1.0 yet," he reminds me. "The biggest challenge we still have is a way for people to buy Dogecoin easily. We need a service like Coinbase. Most people, unless they mine, are getting their Doge by way of the Dogetipbot."

Josh thinks that Doge may reach a higher value compared to more traditional currencies - after all, we both say at the same time, 1 Doge will always be 1 Doge. But he doesn't seen the coin or the community getting any less silly.

"You want seriousness?" he asks. "Cryptocurrency offers such convenience. The fees are minimal. You have the ability to pay instantly. There are a few merchants discussing Dogecoin who will be taking Doge."

The moon is that elusive destination that every shibe aspires to reach. Josh does, too.

"Every says 'to the moon,'" he smiles. Chester shifts and stretches on Josh's shoulders. "It's the unifying phrase. It unites us all. It means so many things to so many people. I see it as more people using Doge, because the more that use it, the better the stability of the network. We have some exciting services in store, services that move beyond Reddit. We're always looking to promote any site that is willing to expand with us - we'll bring the tipbot there."

- Birdie

BUY · SELL · TRADE
MEET · CONNECT

VERIFICATION for YOU

THE
FUTURE
IS HERE

POLI POLI

SHIBE OF THE MONTH

POLI

Dear Readers,

I came here one Sunday night. It was raining outside, and it was cold in weather. I was stuck behind my computer, bored browsing the internet. When I was chatting with somebody from a minecraft server I used to play on, I heard the word BITCOIN. I had heard about this before, but I hadn't really checked on it. So I checked on it, and I thought it was awesome. But by the second I went to their reddit, I was immediately disappointed. There was no friendliness, no happiness, just investors.

That's so boring.

I thought they called it magical internet money.

All they wanted was to invest and earn more. As a person who is annoyed by people that just want more money, I thought this was terrible, so I decided to see if there were any friendly alternatives. What I found, was dogecoins.

This same day, the 16th of March, the doge4water foundation had just been successfully funded. I could see the friendliness in your texts. It was all thank you and giving and ... dogetipbot was just so beautiful.

So I had decided that this would be what I would focus on. I created a wallet and started mining, but it quick showed that even though I was under an hour old, people would "tip" me coins, without me even asking! I still mined though, and when I saw people tipping me I decided that this would be me at some point, so I decided to keep mining just so that I could give back what I had been given.

I also would like to say that for weeks before that night I have had sleeping problems, but that night I went to bed being happy, because I had just been given something of value. I don't care what the prices are.

I don't care if I don't become rich. 1 dogecoin = 1 dogecoin. And whatever I am given, if it is a word, a tip, a sentence - it means something to me.

Thank you dogecoin community, for what you have given to me. It is priceless to me.

Thank you so much, shibes..

Poli

Tip Poli ->

TOM BOICE

> **"Kanye West" immediately demonstrates that Atmosphere hasn't lost their taste for bucking convention"**

Welcome!

I will be using this column to bring you a variety of albums that I feel demand attention, but today I wanted to highlight one of my favorite artists and their latest single release.

The Minnesota based group Atmosphere has loomed large in independent hip-hop for over fifteen years. This is due, in part, to the group's producer Ant who is talented at marrying melody with hard-hitting beats; but it is frontman Slug's poetic verses that give their music nearly infinite replayability.

After taking some time to focus on family and their record label, Rhymesayers, Atmosphere is ready to release their next album, *Southersiders*, on May 1st. Earlier this week, they allowed their fans a sneak peak at the album by releasing a song many were curious about - "Kanye West."

"Kanye West" immediately demonstrates that Atmosphere hasn't lost their taste for bucking convention, opening by asking the listener to "put your hands in the air like you really do care." While Atmosphere has always revelled in going against traditional hip-hop themes, "Kanye West" demonstrates that Slug has not ventured outside of his own comfort-zone, with lyrics that detail a struggling and passionate relationship between himself and an allegorized woman.

The women of Slug's lyrics have represented many things over his career; faith, alcoholism, and music. But in "Kanye West," his discussion of the woman ventures into a territory prolific rappers like Eminem and Jay Z discuss often - the hip-hop industry and their legacy within it.

This may be the reason for the use of "Kanye West" in the song as a descriptor of a person or action overcome by passion. West is well known for being passionate to the point of self-destruction, often acting out in public in ways that cause his image more harm than good. The use of this phrase in the song at once calls to mind passion and legacy.

Lyrical Discussion

At the end of the first verse, Slug and the woman make a trip to Reno, a destination tied to entertainment - but not as mainstream as Vegas.

> Buzz got lose and we're here trying to catch it
> She said that she was unimpressed,
> that's when I stood up and did the Kanye West.

Relating this mystery woman to "the industry," the lyrics here fit within a theme Slug has visited often in songs like "GodLovesUgly" when he says "been paying dues for a decade plus / before that I was just another face on the bus." For Slug, there is no relation between the means and the ends, simply pursuing the ends is enough to fill a life.

This time around though, Slug is looking back on his struggle to build a legacy, and realizes that the struggle was his legacy:

> And right then we started building a team
> Trying to make a better perfect, a little purpose
> The only thing for certain is the sleep disturbance
> But every since people started measuring time
> We've been looking for an easy way to settle our mind
>
> [...]
>
> But when I die put on your Sunday best
> and throw your hands in the air like Kanye West

Verdict

Ant's production on "Kanye West" demonstrates that he has kept up with the times, with a rock-inspired loop that could easily have Kid Cudi rapping over it, but a gothic harmony infused in the rhythm definitely captures the classic "Atmosphere" essence.

While Slug's lyrics have little to contribute to the world today, and show no artistic experimentation, they do demonstrate that he is still the master of his wheelhouse. Metaphor, wordplay, and allegory are Slug's playthings, and who am I to ask for more than that?

I, for one, look forward to the full album, and will be playing "Kanye West" every day until it comes out. If you are looking for that "new" hip-hop, steer clear of Atmosphere and check out Schoolboy Q's Oxymoron.

Tip Tom
->

TOM BOICE

AUTODOGE

AUTODOGE INTERVIEWS DOGECOIN NASCAR DESIGNER RYAN, AKA /U/WIDOWMAKERXLS

AD: First and foremost, thank you very much for taking the time to take part in an interview with the very first Dogecoin magazine, **Very Much Wow**! Introduce yourself to us and tell us a bit about who you are, where you're from, and what you do.

RH: Thanks for having me! When I am not /u/WidowmakerXLS , I am known as Ryan. I am originally from Pennsylvania, about 15 miles northeast of Philadelphia. I am a proud graduate of The West Chester University of Pennsylvania (Go Rams!) These days I am living in a western suburb of Philly. When I am not redditing, I work in the exciting field of television production, specifically live sporting events. I don't have any formal training or professional experience with graphical design. All of my work is done in my spare time, often only for my own personal enjoyment and the enjoyment of others. At one point in my life I was really interested in making graphic design a career path for me, but in life, things are always changing!

AD: Do you have any background with or interest in NASCAR and its events?

RH: I have been a NASCAR fan since the mid-90s. My first memories are of watching Dale Earnhardt Sr. win the 1994 championship. I loved his style, his attitude, and his image. Ever since his tragic death, I have been a big Dale Jr. fan! I have been to several races over the years at Dover. NASCAR is a great community that both divides and unites large groups of people, which to me is what sports are all about! As for Dogecoin, while I can't recall the first time I heard of it, I became interested in the community back when they helped to send the Jamacan bobsled team to the Sochi Olympic games! I think its awesome how a group of people can gather for a common cause and make things happen that otherwise would not! I find the culture quirky and unique, which I think is great!

My design is the result of many hours of work and lots and lots of coffee! From the very beginning, I wanted to create something that a) Represented the Dogecoin community in the best and most professional way possible, b) Was something that Josh and Phil would be excited to run, and c) Look badass and standout on the track! My original design was gold in color, but after reading many comments from the community, I decided to do a black version to keep with the current scheme that Josh and Phil run.

I constantly combed the posts and comments, trying to include as many things as I could on the car without making it too cluttered. This was no easy task! There were so many good ideas from the users that it was very hard for me to pick what made the cut and what didn't. This scheme was truly designed not just by me, but by the entire community!

AD: Your design was chosen by the community from a contest between competitors. In this contest, many other designs showed both promise and merit. From these designs, what elements did you like most?

RH: All of the designs were great. Any of the other 5 designs would have looked just as good as mine on the track. I knew from the very beginning that I would have to come in with the best possible design possible. I knew that there were going to be several other great designs.

I love the gold and white combo on /u/Captain_Frylock design. He really nailed the color combos on the base. /u/NukacolaV3 put together a great design as well. Really loved his

1:42:820

colors. I loved /u/joe_designs car as well. I actually didn't vote for my own
design. I voted for /u/Captain_Frylock !

I'd like to thank the other designers for making this contest so competitive! The more good designs you have, the better the final product becomes!

AD: You've mentioned to the community that you "work in the television industry." In that industry, what was your experience like? Do you feel this experience has in any way helped shape your work as a designer?

RH: I currently work in television production, specifically in the production of live sports. It is an awesome field to work in! I get to wake up and go to sporting events for a living and see a lot of the behind the scenes things that the average fan doesn't have access to. As a huge sports fan, I couldn't think of anything I would rather be doing with my career. I work with a ton of great people who make my job a ton of fun.

AD: What part of the car was your favorite part on which to work, and what part do you think turned out the best?

RH: This one is easy! The rear of the car is by far my favorite element of the design. It happened by accident too. My original plan featured just text, "much draft," "very push," and "to the moon!" I was working on the hood logo and copied the shibe-head into the file from another document. It happened to appear on the rear and it just clicked for me! There was no going back!

AD: Each designer has his or her own creative process. Step by step, take us through your own. What do you like most and least about this process? Has this process changed throughout the years?

RH: For me personally, I am all about trial and error. I have never been about sketching designs, rather I just go with my gut. If I decide what I am doing isn't working, I start over! I went through around 10 different designs for the base paint on the dogecar before coming up with the final version. Once something clicks though, the ideas just keep coming.

You really gain momentum when you start getting excited about a design. The hardest thing for me sometimes is knowing when to stop. It's so easy to infinitely add things to a design and before you know it, it is a cluttered mess! Less truly is often more!

My favorite thing about the process is seeing something go from a thought in my head to a finished product. You really get a warm fuzzy feeling when you finally reach the finish line. My least favorite part of the process is the time-requirements. As you can imagine, checking every little thing adds a ton of time to the process!

A HUGE thank you to Josh Wise and Phil Parsons for their willingness to be involved in this! Thanks to everyone who is currently working behind the scenes to help my deign come to life! Thank you to everyone who contributed! You should be proud of yourselves.

What is happening is an unprecedented event in NASCAR. A crowd-funded car is an incredible achievement! This could open many new ways for race-teams to get on track, which, as a NASCAR fan, is awesome.

Thank you to /u/Iamamafia and /u/Moolah_ for putting this contest together! Thank you to everyone who voted, not just for me, but for any of the great designs. Thanks to the other designers for putting out kick-ass schemes!

A special shoutout Andy and Ice_Man over at SimRacingDesign for the renders of my car, and to /u/Captain_Frylock for recommending me to them! I'm sure I'm forgetting many others, but thank you to anyone who contributed to this process! Go Josh!

Let's see this car in victory lane on May 4th!!!

THERE'S OUR SHIBE

GO JOSH
We can't wait to cheer Josh Wise on in the big NASCAR race!

JOSH WISE: #98

SINCE 2013
DOGECOIN

VROOOOOM

PERFORMANCE

Tip autodoge ->

WOW MUCH TALK

DANIEL LILJEBERG

THE CRAIGSLIST OF DOGECOIN | SUCHLIST.COM

SuchList.com is where Doge is King, according to founder Daniel Liljeberg. The site provides a venue for Dogecoin users across the world to sell any kind of good and service you can imagine in exchange for Doge. SuchList.com also provides space for community listings such as events and carpool requests.

Daniel is passionate about transparency. His site requires users to go through a verification process in order to provide another level of security. SuchList.com prominently displays a message regarding the use of cookies at the site, and invites the visitor to accept of decline them.

Daniel talked with VMW about SuchList.com and his vision for Dogecoin. You will love this. Daniel is a true Shibe.

- Birdie

VMW: How did you first learn about Dogecoin?

DL: My first contact with Dogecoin was a post on the forum of the Swedish site sweclockers.com. I had just gotten into Litecoin after, like many, "missing the train" of Bitcoin. I remember reading about Bitcoin and some part of my brain remembered that I bought about $10 worth of Bitcoin a long time ago. But I had no idea where they were. After understanding how much that would have been worth today I was damn sure I was going to get in on the Litecoin thing

I almost raised a lot of money and built a large mining farm due to people in my surroundings wanting to get in on it too, but after going through the state of digital currencies and the absolute outpour of new coins, I decided that it would be too risky at that point. Although I felt Litecoin would rise in value due to all the other people wanting to make a quick profit, I felt it was too volatile to risk other

people's money. So I advised them against it, and settled for building a dedicated miner at home and letting it mine away.

So this was when I read that post about Dogecoin. So my inital though was, "another one?... Jesus Christ!". I ended up on the Dogecoin subreddit and something just clicked. Here were the advocates of the latest addition to digital currencies, based on a damn joke, and they seemed to get it. They understood what was important for the possible success of digital currencies as a whole. They didn't seem interested in becoming rich or hoarding and cashing out on a high. They worked to spread information, advocate the use of Dogecoin, keeping coins in circulation, helping new people get into the coin and also using it to do good things.

By not taking their own coin so seriously they had done what should have been done for digital currencies as a whole a long time ago and had actually, probably without knowing it, become a terrific PR machine. Not necessarily for Dogecoin alone, but for the entire idea of digital currencies.

When I saw this dedication, commitment and burning desire to "do it right" I couldn't just wave them off as crazy people worshiping a dog meme (sorry Doge). They were in fact closer to understanding the entire thing than anyone I had talked to before. Introducing a revolutionary way for people pay for things won't be possible if everyone who's involved in it just wants to get rich quick.

I walked upstairs, opened the door to the room where my miner stood, shut the miner down and reconfigured it to mine Dogecoins. I have never looked back since. Before I looked daily at the value of Litecoin. "Did I make my investment back yet?" and so on. Now, I don't worry at all about the relational value of Dogecoin to other coins.

Dogecoin has the one thing that

Daniel Liljeberg of SuchList.com

is truly important for an experiment such as this to succeed. A strong and dedicated following. That was what I wanted to be part of, changing the world. Not making quick money.

VMW: Why did you start SuchList.com?

DL: Bartering, commerce... these things have always applied value to things. Commerce brings stability and value to a currency since you know that you can accept the given currency as payment and then in turn use it to purchase other goods and service that you desire.

How do we best achive this? Sure, we can walk around asking businesses to accept Dogecoin. But I felt there was something with greater impact that we could do right now. We could decide to start accepting it as means of payment among ourselves. The Dogecoin subreddit had around 60K subscribers at that time and the number grew every day. If we all decided to accept Dogecoin, the power in that change is quite extraordinary. In fact, if the entire world turned their back on Dogecoin, 60K people using it among themselves would still give it a real world value.

I wanted to focus on making it easy for users to find each other and do business. I decided to keep the site free to use and not charge a percentage or fee for as long as possible. I understand that it's a utopian dream to think I can do this forever, but for now donations by the wonderful community are keeping things going.

I decided to make sure that ads on the site could be easily filtered on different countries, regions or cities so it would be possible for a user to find someone in his own town to meet and do business with. My hope was that this might bring people of the community together and some of these meetings might blossom into local Dogecoin activities etc.

Although people have told me to monetize this, my reason for starting Such-Listcom is that I want to help the Dogecoin community and help Dogecoin succeed as an actual usable currency.

VMW: What different countries have members at SuchList.com?

DL: There are registered users from Australia, Brazil, Canada, China, Czech Republic, Denmark, France, Germany, Honduras, India, Ireland, Italy, Lithuania, Mexico, Netherlands, New Zeland, Portugal, Russia, Slovakia, Sweden, Turkey, United Kingdom and United States.

We have returning visitors from as many as 107 countries including Palestine, Zimbabwe, Uruguay, Jordan, Belize and on and on.

During the few weeks we have existed (which is probably a lot in the Dogecoin world) we have had ~7.000 unique visitors and 43.000 pages viewed. The average visit lasts over 3 minutes so there seem to be real interest in doing business with Dogecoin. On an avereg day SuchList.com recives about 4-500 unique visitors.

VMW: What are some of the unusual items that a person can find for sale at SuchList.com?

DL: When the first ad was posted I was very excited and remeber saying "One day we might even see a car for sale in Dogecoins on the site." It was half a joke and half a wish that Dogecoin might make it there in a few years. Now a few weeks later there are two cars listed on the site and if you happen to be in Italy and find yourself in need of a boat that is also possible to sort out with Dogecoins.

VMW: Tell us about your new validation program.

DL: With any gold rush comes people without much care for others than themselves who want to grab as much as they can by any means. Dogecoin and other digital currencies are no exception. We have seen it time and time again with people being scammed in online markets and online exchanges getting hacked.

This is extremely damaging to the entire notion of digital currencies. It's hard to promote them and say they are safe when at the same time millions is reported stolen in form of digital currencies.

I know a lot of people work very hard on making good services for Dogecoin and unlocking all the great potential of Dogecoin. But you still can't help wondering how many people have just stitched a service together, thrown it up onto a web server and charging a percentage or fee to be able to get a piece of the pie before it's to late and left security out cold.

If a person is able to look at validated information of a user they are about to do business with they can use this information when making the decision of whether they should trust the individual or not. I sat down and built a generic validation system that I could then add different validators to.

The validators that are live on the site today are: SMS, Reddit, Twitter and Website.

They connect the user to a given phone number verified via SMS, to a Reddit account, Twitter account or Website. They all require the user to follow steps to make sure that they have access to the given account and then the system validates this fact.

This information is then presented on a users public profile page and links can take users to the validated Twitter, Website or Redit account in question. This allow people to easily look into the history of a user and use that information in his decision making. If a user created his Reddit account four days ago and has only been posting about torrent sites I might be a bit wary. But if the user has been active on Reddit for years and never had any complaints I would probably feel much more secure. More sensitive data such as phone numbers are masked before being presented to avoid a user getting phone calls he might not want.

VMW: What does "The Moon" mean to you?

DL: "The Moon" for me probably symbolizes the very rudemenatry idea of "making it as a functional digital currency." No digital currency has really done that yet. Bitcoin has almost been there, but there has been too much speculation involved in Bitcoin to keep it stable so people can't trust it. It's hard to sell something for payment in a coin you know could be worth half as much tomorrow.

So reaching a stable value and good circulation and usage... that's the moon ;)

> "When I saw this dedication, commitment and burning desire to "do it right" I couldn't just wave them off as crazy people worshiping a doge meme (sorry Doge). They were in fact closer to understanding the entire thing than anyone I had talked to before."

The Shibe Mint

DOGE Eshop .COM

DogeMovies.com

REDBOX with DOGE!

LEARN ABOUT DOGECOIN

DOGE FEVER

wow

WWW.REDDIT.COM/R/DOGECOIN

7QUESTIONS FOR GOODSHIBE

You Do the Math →

VMW: How did you first hear about Dogecoin? What did you think?

GS: I heard about Dogecoin very early on, actually. I started mining on a lark around day 2 or so, but I've got a tiny little videocard. I tried supplementing my coins by buying in... during the the first big spike. Not long after buying in, I watched in horror as it started to drop... a lot. When it finally settled in around 80 satoshis I was like 'It's not going to go any further!' so I bought in again... and watched it drop to 30. So yeah, my first thoughts were very positive... until the crash. Then I kind of freaked out. On the bright side, that lead me to discovering the Dogecoin community, so I figure it all worked out.

VMW: What prompted you to start Wolves and Weasels?

GS: I started Of Wolves and Weasels back when we were either still in or just recovering from 30 satoshis - my very first post was about trying to stop what I'd perceived as the 'DOGEpocalypse' - where our coin would get devalued so much that people could just swoop in and buy hundreds of millions of DOGE for 1 BTC. I saw the pressure from Multipools and all sorts as putting lots of pressure on our valuation so I had created the post to try and convince my fellow Shibes to Mine Defensively - to raise the global hashrate and help make it unprofitable for multipools to hop on and strip-mine our coin (auto-sell DOGE for BTC, without care of the current valuation).

I think it is still relevant because it reminds, well, it reminds me that we must be ever-vigilant. The good outnumber the bad by a large margin, but we must never forget that they are there and be aware of that. Lots of good Shibes

have lost a lot of coins to Predators (Wolves) and Scammers (Weasels).

VMW: Where do you see Doge evolving over the next year? Five years?

GS: Dogecoin has the potential to become the next generation of 'appreciation' - the ability for people to easily show support, financially, for the goods and services and arts that they appreciate -- to, essentially, empower creators to create more of what they like   is a truly world-changing advancement. Other coins, technically, can do this - but they aren't. I liken it to having the tools but choosing not to use them.

Because of Dogecoin's unique social and psychological makeup, these ideas - our values - push us to show appreciation for others, to share our DOGEs and inspire others.And I think it's been quite successful, actually.

VMW: Do you think Dogecoin and other cryptos will change the world?

GS: Absolutely. Dogecoin especially. Why? Because we have the will. Like I said earlier, any other coin could do what we do. The difference is that we're doing it. Consistently. We've enshrined it as part of our Ethos. We take great pride in being proactive, in sharing and making positive, fun, change in the world. That doesn't take tech, that takes desire. A need.

VMW: What does "The Moon" mean to you?

GS: I think this post sums it up the best: http://www.reddit.com/r/dogecoin/comments/1x2yfx/of_wolves_and_weasels_day_29_the_moon_in_all_its/

VMW: What's the one story you haven't yet told?

GS: That's an excellent question - I'm not sure yet. I often pick my stories on the morning of, when I first wake up I take a look at the community and see what catches my eye. Every post is written that morning, while its fresh in my head. The story I really can't wait to tell is the one that truly launches our rocket, the one that sets us rocketing off into the mainstream. It's coming... probably later this summer.

VMW: What do you think is the Dogecoin community's best achievement to date?

GS: Our heart. Seriously, having and maintaining a beating heart behind our coin - caring about something other than naked profit... it's truly helped to set us apart from the 200+ other crypto coins. There are others working hard to try and be us, to mimic us and more... but you can't fake 'giving a damn'. Our coin is a rag-tag collection of all the best kinds of people on the internet. All those fantastic people who ever wanted to be a part of something bigger than themselves; who wanted their voice, their actions to matter and reverberate forward... and mean something. Dogecoin is doing what it's doing, making waves, changing lives, inspiring the world... because we want it to. And if that isn't an achievement worth being proud of... I don't know what is.

EDGARBOUNDS

INTRODUCING A DOGECOIN HUMOR COLUMN TO THE FAMILY

[An account of encounters on the subject of becoming a humor writer for The Official Dogecoin Magazine: Very Much Wow, based on true stories]

[Excitedly telling my mother:]

Mom, I just got an email from somebody I met on Reddit today. GUESS WHAT?! I'm. going. to be a humor writer for The Official Dogecoin Magazine: Very Much Wow!

"Reddi?"

Uh, it's a place where... young men go to be ridiculous and terrible with semi-anonymity? But it's more too. Like a lot of stuff happens there. And on the dogcoin place we do a lot of good stuff.

[Author pronounces it dog-coin to outsiders for clarity's sake.]

And we don't get into trouble; there's mostly a lot of believing and waiting and comical serendipity. It's a lot like Waiting for Godot. ... Just forget I said anything about it, just you would be proud I'm a part of it?

"Now what is a dog-coin? You know your mother doesn't do dogs. If you try to bring another dog to visit this house..."

No mom, it's only a little bit about dogs. Like this one dog. A picture of him. He looks funny like he's thinking and he knows something but he's also afraid too. It's kinda like the Mona Lisa for our generation."

"The magazine is about a picture of a dog?"

Not quite. It's about a "cryp-to-currency" based on that dog. So that's like a distributed, digital currency... Like a better alternative to US dollars. I-it has the potential to disrupt the financial sector as we know it and bring important parts of government back to the people and help the poor and disenfranchised!"

"Oh my God, I have raised an anarchist! Oh baby, please don't get up with those people who light cars on fire and get shot by the police. You will drive your poor mother crazy!"

Mom. Mom! I swear we don't do stuff like that. We help the Jamaican bobsled team go to the olympics, and provide african kids drinking water, and promote goodness and generosity and happiness, and sponsor Nascars, and raise money for cancer and AIDS research, and support each other when there are thieves about and and...

"... ..."

Really Mom! You are just going to trust me on this one.

"Well but you have been talking to people on the internet?! Don't you know how dangerous that is? Don't you watch the news?"

[Telling my Uncle Tim]

Boy, you into *that stuff*, ain't you!

[He means drugs if that is not clear.]

[Communicating to my dog, Belle, that we are not going to bed even though it's bedtime]

No Belle, not yet, we have a column right now! Your pops is a writer.

[Dog begins to get excited at some subconscious excited twinkle in my voice, irregular bursts of tail wagging begin while she looks at my face trying to contemplate it, figure it out.]

"MAGAZINE, Belle! WRITER!", I shout as only a happy, dog and doge loving idiot in the privacy of his own company can.. "That's right, girl!

[Tail begins oscillating at speed sufficient to wag dog, full blown excitement. She has latched onto the emphasized word "writer" as the important part of this excitement. But what is "writer"? Is it like "walk"? Walk is pretty sweet. Is it like "bath"--no, shit, "bath" is one of the bad ones. Is it like "treat"? I bet it's like treat. I love treat. But it's not treat... OH GOD, is it better than treat?! What can be better than treat? How does? What even--]

Meanwhile having seen her wheels turning, I have gotten out of the chair to reinforce this excitement and send it spiraling up. I know what needs to be done. I slowly bend down to bring my face to the level of her frantic gaze and contort my face in such away that I'm clearly either about to speak very loudly or dislodge something from my throat (imagine you were just about to yell "BOO" to scare somebody from the opposite side of a football stadium and you wanted to time it just right so he would throw his popcorn into an interesting place).

She knows what's next. I always put her through this rigmarole. I'm about to reveal the game. Say an important word that will make all this curiosity suddenly make sense to her. Whether it be "treat", "dogpark", "dinner", "outside" or what. Her eyes are practically watering. She's starting to growl and she's bent down in the front with her forelegs outstretched in a playful attack posture.

My face is probably reddening just a little bit from the strain of holding the face. She's gonna lose it! I might too--"Dog and man die in freak twin aneurysm!" But no finally as I reach just a few inches from her face I let it go: "Dogecoin!"

"BARK!" and run and look at me. "BARK!" and run and look at me. Crazy circuits around the office furniture ensue. She could be a Nascar. This must be something good she must think, because I sure am happy and excited about it.

"DOGECOIN!" I say again louder to confirm when she looks at me. She is in a state beyond pleased. Practically, she has no idea why. Regardless, she has just opened Pokemon on her 9th birthday, she has just won both showcases on the Showcase Showdown.

I am laughing and excited and entertained and we just feed off of each other for an unreasonable amount of time. "Dogecoin", I say. "Dogecoin! Dogecoin! Dogecoin!"

Tip Edgar ->

PRIME DIRECTIVE: MOON

SUCH SPACE

SO WARP

DOGE AFTER DARK

email DogeAfterDark@VeryMuchWow.com with your midnight rantings and moonlit thoughts...

Middle of the night crazy ideas... Are your legs twitching while you dream? Do you feel like howling at the moon? Send us your Doge After Dark Dreams and Moonlit Ideas.
To get things started, a popular, but choosing to remain anonymous, www.reddit.com/r/dogecoin member had this interesting "Stray Doge" thought...

I was imagining what would happen if Doge becomes "THE" virtual currency of the world. All of those cultures, all of those countries! Will the meme survive? Is one breed enough for the entire globe? Would other breeds stage a coup? The Poodle Rebellion?

Beyond that, even if Doge becomes THE Currency, there will be others. Will competing memes be humanity's greatest achievement? Doge has been victorious over fedoras, cats of various species, and penguins. Will this hold true?

Imagine a currency that doesn't call itself a coin. Maybe it calls itself a "vector," like something from another dimension. Which brings me to another idea. Aliens. Do they already use virtual currencies? Is this what will bring about First Contact?

For that matter, who is Satoshi Nakamoto? Is he from Earth? Or did he land at Roswell? (My apologies to the New Mexican editor of this publication. It's the fracken middle of the night and I'm on my second bottle of wine.)

Would like to hear back from other Earthlings and Redditors (not the same thing most days) who want to share their thoughts.

Dear Mr. Doge,

My miner is in heat. What do I do?

Signed,
To Hot to Handle

Dear Thinks He's Hot,

Do you mean "miner" or do you mean miner? If the former, I suggest you chill out on some Barry White and vanilla ice cream. Not chocolate, bad for doges.
If you mean the latter, try wagging your tail in its general direction, laying it out on cold concrete in the shade with good rawhide bone, or, how about taking it on a quick run through a sprinkler system?

Dear Mr. Doge,

My gf is really into the doge meme, but she still doesn't get Dogecoins. She has all of these tacky doge meme posters taped up around her bedroom. One of them is even wearing a red beret and smoking a hand-rolled cigarette! When we're getting friendly, if my eyes are open, those damned doges are staring at me, and when my eyes are closed, all I can think about is my hashrate. What do I do?

Signed,
Reaching the end of my leash

DOGE
ASK A

"I'm just a hot-blooded American Shibe. Got trouble? I give YOU the tips! "

email askadoge @verymuchwow.com with your sadness...

SUCH AMAZE ADVICE

<- Tip
Ask A Doge

Dear Reaching Too Far,

Number one. One eye open, one eye closed, see what happens. Might even turn her on. Two. Ask her if you can put a poster up explaining Dogecoin. Tell her it's for her, but it's really for you. Nothing like the blockchain to get your heart racing. Three. Get a pet-friendly motel room.

Dear Ask A Doge,

I am of the feline persuasion. My human, Bob, started mining Dogecoins three months ago. Now he's a dogeillionaire and thinks that dogs are awesome. (Which of course they are not.) Unfortunately kittehcoin has not taken off. What can I do?

Signed,
Catbox Blues

Dear CB,

One. Don't be so down on the opposite species. If it wasn't for them, you wouldn't be an opposite species, which would take half the fun out of your life. Two. A million dogecoins won't buy what it used to a couple of weeks ago, but you can probably get a can of Fancy Feast. (What would a million kittehcoins get you? Huh?) Number three says it all. Menage-a-trois?

There once was a Shibe,
Who wanted to go to the moon.
But alas, no Dogecoin, said the Shibe.
...But he would find a way to the moon.

He asked the community,
Who were tipping constantly!
When the Shibe asked them...
They said the only way was being a team.

So the Shibe worked with the other Shi-
bes...
And all went well,
So this story, passed down from Shibe to
Shibe...
Was always so wow.

Cameron

There once was a shibe named kadoodle
Who was a bit wet in the noodle
He'd leap all about
While is Family would shout
"Kadoodle, you're a shibe, not a poodle!"

Dave Smith

A dogecoin can cause much excite-
Tips, love, and humor that's light.
With a community so strong,
How could Shibes go wrong?
Together, our future is bright!

D Rowley

There once was a Shibe based money.
At first they just though it was funny.
And now they all swoon
as we fly to the moon,
For that Shibe the future much sunny.

Charlie

There was once a shibe in Wow-ville.
Who lived a much great life, but still.
When he wanted to tip
For the water he sipped
He couldn't pay for it, not even a nip.
So using the bones he got from a loin
He created the currency called dogecoin
Now all the shibes and humans alike
Take flight to the moon on a rocket with a spike
Tips a plenty is the dogecoin way
Now let's give dogecoin a hip-hip-hooray!

Peyton Piscioneri

There once was a shibe with a
dream.
Some thought him only a meme.
With his friends by his side,
Filled with joy and with pride,
They went to the moon as a team.

many words

COMMUNITY
THE ONLY PAGE WITH ALL COMIC SANS!

A bulldog en route to the bank
With a big bag of cash and some coins that would clank
Saw a sight that perplexed
Just as sure as it vexed
(As a bulldog, you see, is a crank)

Before him, a wild affair –
Cream colored dogs that would prance without care!
Sure, they danced, sang and talked,
But the thing that most shocked:
They were throwing their coins in the air!

The bulldog said, "How do you live?
Don't you see that your pocket's as good as a sieve?
My lot is for *me*.
I'm entitled, you see"
But the Shibes just continued to give

A kind Shibe then took note and spoke up
"Let me give you a tip, in a cup.
Now listen with care,
That cup's yours, hoard or share,
With that, welcome aboard my good pup!"

Now, a bulldog is known for his grip
But that day saw his crankiness slip
He let go of his greed;
As a Shibe, he was freed!
"To the moon!" he says now, "Have a tip!"

Martholomule

WOW

There was shibe named Doge
All with great power he arose
With his power in wealth. DogeCoins, made in Beijing.
And as to his people he said one only thing
"TO THE MOON" he cheered as he blasted off into space – with his glamorous pose.

Zachary Z Toothman

There
once was a scribe without coin who
tried ever so hard not to whine But
when he got doged'
He got lots of courage
And 'to the moon' he encouraged

Foulnut

There once was a shibe from the moon
All the other shibes that saw him would swoon
They did not know
For this future shibe
Charity would be such a boon.

Max Conser

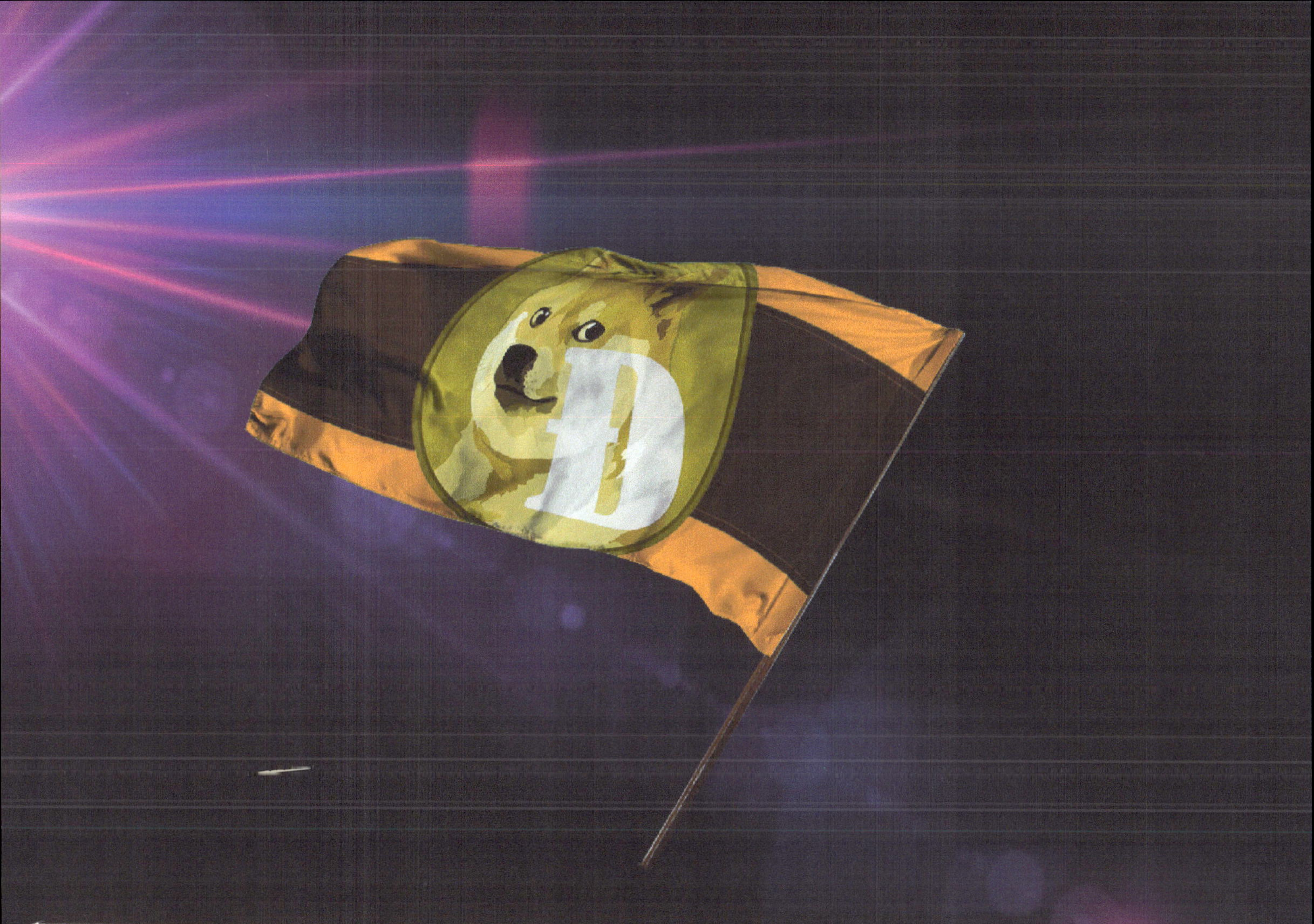

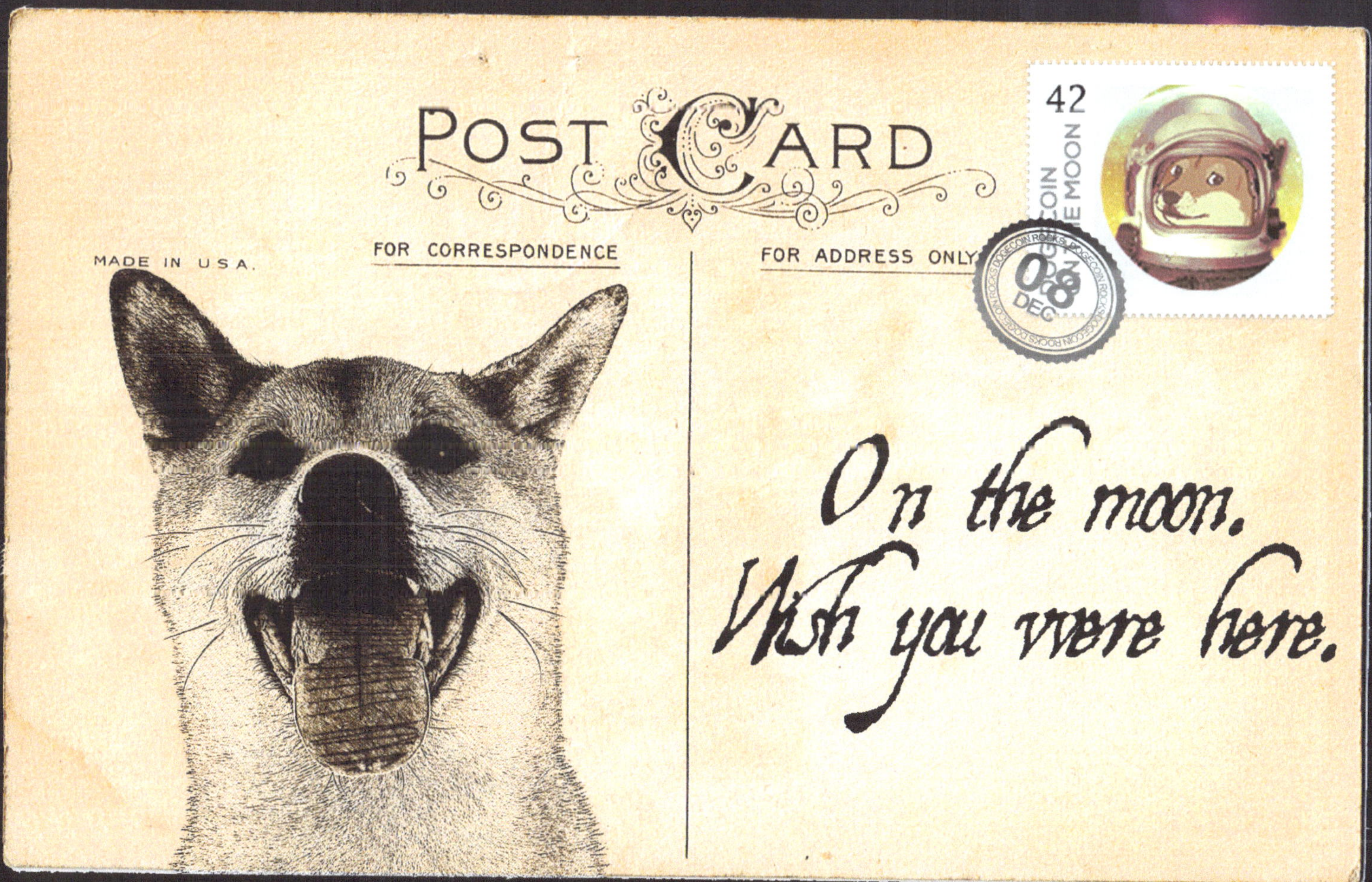

POST CARD

MADE IN U.S.A.

FOR CORRESPONDENCE

FOR ADDRESS ONLY

On the moon.
Wish you were here.